THE IMPLANTED WORD

Therefore lay aside all filthiness and overflow of wickedness, and receive with meekness the implanted word, which is able to save your souls.

—James 1:21 (NKJV)

ARLETTE TEJEDA

ISBN 979-8-88751-422-2 (paperback)
ISBN 979-8-88751-423-9 (digital)

Christian Faith Publishing
832 Park Avenue
Meadville, PA 16335
www.christianfaithpublishing.com

Printed in the United States of America

Dedication

I dedicate this book to my mother, children, and a suffering generation battling with the effects of trauma, mental health, feeling stuck, and the fear of never becoming the best version of self.

In the many battles of your life, I saw the wounds of your soul, and though I was too young to fully understand. Soon the day would come when I would have to face my own, and it was then that in my pain, I felt your pain and understood your suffering. Your story and mine are the drivers that have propelled this book with the intent to help others heal.

Mami, en mi corazón vives por siempre (in my heart you live forever)…

You made me strong and relentless. There was no place for fear or thoughts of defeat; my only option was to overcome, not for me but for you. The immense feeling of love blended with responsibility helped me overcome many hardships and challenges.

Thank you for your love, honor, support, and admiration even when I was clueless and did not know what in the world I was doing.

Ashley, Kaila, and Ismael Jr., you will always be my precious babies…

CONTENTS

PREFACE

Overcoming darkness, times of despair, trauma, and feelings of worthlessness is not easy and may seem almost impossible. My greatest hope is to shine a light into those dark places to help you see that healing for your soul is attainable no matter how deep your wounds are.

I am hopeful that as you turn the pages of this book, your heart and soul will be healed, and your spirit awakened. In addition, you'll be equipped with the power tools needed to free your soul from anything, keeping it hostage.

If you are willing to open your heart and believe the Truth I share in this book, then you will be saved, healed, transformed, and empowered to walk out your God given purpose while experiencing the best version of YOU!

OPENING PRAYER

Heavenly Father, I pray this book serves as a healing guide for the reader. Please, Lord, enlighten the eyes of their understanding, awaken their spirit, heal their heart, and save their soul. Lord, please create in them an immense hunger to pursue their life purpose and calling in You, Lord. Give them grace and favor for the journey; open divine doors; prosper them; and give them joy, peace, and a sense of fulfillment as they embark on their healing journey. Lord, I declare them saved, healed, and transformed. We thank You Lord for the finished work.

In Jesus mighty name, I pray. Amen!

THE TRUTH WILL SET YOU FREE

Jesus said to him, I am the way, the truth, and the life.
No one comes to the Father except through Me.

—John 14:6 (NKJV)

The Truth I am about to share with you is going to give you a new and powerful perspective, one that is bound to shake you to the core and transform your life as it did mine.

For several years now, I have been on a journey of self-discovery, mostly trying to find this thing called "purpose." In the pursuit of purpose, I found something much more important. I found my true essence and the healing of my soul. It is true that if one has no soul, one has no life. It is just as true that a damaged soul will prevent you from living your best life and that would be contrary and a total defeat of one's "purpose." I also learned that it is very possible to exist while not truly living because the fullness of life is only accomplished in a purpose-filled life.

If you are anything like me, you are relentless, hardworking, ambitious, and always dreaming of conquering the world. But for some reason, no matter what I did, I could only soar so high, eventually taking a downward spiral that would cause me to stay stuck for a long time. My efforts were constantly being overwhelmed by the rapidly increasing number of challenges. As the years went by, my frustration intensified, and the thought of not ever becoming the best version of "me" haunted the very core of my being. I became so sick of being sick and tired! Despite the condition I was in, there was a drive within me that never died, so I kept getting up and showing up!

Soon I discovered there were areas in my being that were suffering from malnutrition. I learned that malnutrition does not only happen to the physical body, but it also happens to one's spirit and soul. For better understanding, my spirit and soul were lacking the proper nutrients that promote health and growth.

It was evident that I was capable of soaring since I had accomplished it many times before and indeed possessed many notable gifts. Then why is it that I always end up losing everything I work so hard to obtain? Certainly, the exterior world was not at fault; it was I who played a big role in self-sabotage. But why would I sabotage myself? The answer is lack of knowledge. But I blamed everything and everyone, not knowing the problem was within.

My internal being was in disorder. I was a complete mess, although my outer appearance did not resemble it. My makeup was one of a strong woman, not to mention the problem solver for many. At times, I'd carry the weight of the world on my shoulders. Eventually, it all caught up to me; my inner person was suffering more than I could bear, becoming weaker by the day, and being overtaken by anxiety and depression. Every disappointment, betrayal, failure, and loss fragmented my being. It is no wonder that I was not able to sustain anything if I was completely falling apart.

I began to feel gradual changes and constant conflict within me. So much so, at times, it felt as if there were two of me with different perspectives constantly at war. There was such controversy inside me. I could go from wanting to conquer the world to absolutely wanting to be invisible and completely unseen. This roller coaster went on for several years, debilitating my being. It was at that moment that I knew I was going through some type of imbalance, and acknowledged I needed help. One thing I knew for sure: I was not going to resort to medication or physiatric treatment, not that I don't respect the profession but after seeing my mother's process with mental health, watching her slowly perishing and never having any type of healing—in fact, becoming an addict to prescription medication. I was not going down that path. Instead, I decided to explore many different avenues just to find that the self-help industry is filled with many different belief systems that, at times, are contrary to one another. I just became more confused and discouraged. Then one day, while relentlessly seeking, the Truth found me. I was invited to a church and given a Bible, a Bible that would introduce me to the healer and savior of my soul. In all honesty, the change did not happen right away; as a matter of fact, it got worse before it got better. But it did get better!

When I became a born-again Christian, I began reading the Bible. The Word of God will lead you to all Truth, a Truth that will set you free. At first, I didn't understand much when I read it, but reading the Bible was part of being a Christian, so I read my Bible every day. The more I read, the more interesting it became. Soon it became my favorite book, and boy, oh boy, did the fun begin.

Each day God showed me through His word how much He loves me, and with that same love, He showed me the areas where I had fallen short. Acknowledging my faults, hurts, and traumas was not easy. Many times I'd put up a fight, especially in the area of forgiveness, because forgiving someone who caused you unbearable pain or deceived you and the people you love the most is the hardest thing I had to do. But God, in the kindest and gentlest way, made me understand that unforgiveness was holding me back. Forgiveness was key to the healing of my soul and empowered me to take back my life. There was no way I was going to move forward if I did not learn to forgive and God was not going to leave me hurting, after all, He is the healer of our soul. So I had no choice but to learn to forgive; this process was very painful and, at the same time, overly liberating. Once I genuinely learned the lesson of forgiveness and humbled myself before God, then He began revealing me to me. Can you imagine the Creator of heaven, earth, and everything in it giving me a crash course on my full composition and me realizing I was wonderfully created by the hands of the Master? Every detail, He carefully sought out. This gave me identity and self-worth to know that I am His unique masterpiece and that there is no one else like me. It was inevitable. I became hooked on the Book and completely in love with God.

As I continued my Christian walk, I learned that the Word of God is infallible; it just made more sense each day. As I turned the pages of the Bible, my life turned for the better. Each step I took directed by the Word of God gave me the best results. It wasn't long before I knew God's Word was, is, and will always be the ultimate Truth and the solution to all of our troubles.

I soon began serving in my church and, throughout the years, served in several departments. While every department blessed me with priceless knowledge and experience, the most fulfilling experiences for me happened while evangelizing on the streets. I've been privileged to see God do miracles, signs, and wonders on a street corner and people give their lives to Christ in a parking lot. But I have also seen hunger, homelessness, suffering, pain, addiction, mental illness, and the list goes on. That is why I am eager to share all the knowledge I acquired throughout my healing journey, in hope that people suffering will be healed as I was healed and continue to be healed. If you are alive and breathing, there is still hope!

This journey starts on the inside, and you must be completely convinced that external things are not valuable to this process as your internal being is not nurtured by external things. Therefore, if you are of the idea that having a certain amount of money will better your condition, dispose that idea immediately because it is not going to help you. Money is only effective in the hands of an internally unified person with a clear concept of their life purpose. Other than that, money will be misused. Let's be clear, money can buy you nice things, and it is also necessary for daily living, but it cannot fix your soul. I happen to know very rich messed-up people, and I'm sure you may know some too. The same goes for people, you can't hold people responsible for your happiness, healing, or success. Nothing is responsible for fixing YOU. This responsibility lies solely on you.

Moving forward, you must be ready to confront your ego. You must be willing to tear down the old to build up the new. The only way to find the best you is by completely letting go of your old ways, destructive beliefs adopted, and the ideologies that have affected the outcomes of your life. It is also necessary to dig deep and confront the ugly things from your past as these may be stored in your soul and are longing for proper closure. Once you start to experience inner healing, external changes are inevitable.

This book will give you a biblical breakdown of your full composition. My intention is to help you identify the area(s) in "YOU" that needs attention and healing. In addition to giving you the knowledge needed to restore those areas, and watch you flourish beyond measure.

CHAPTER 1

Welcome to the Unveiling
of Your Being

*Now may the God of peace Himself sanctify you completely;
and may your whole spirit, soul, and body be preserved
blameless at the coming of our Lord Jesus Christ.*

—1 Thess. 5:23 (NKJV)

You are tripartite—a three-part being. Your being is composed of spirit, soul, and body.

You are a spiritual being having an earthly experience, you have a soul that is becoming daily, and you dwell in a physical body that serves as a vehicle to navigate the terrestrial realm.

When you look in the mirror, you see a reflection of your physical body. This is only one part of your being. And while you can dress your body to look stellar on the outside and even have great physical health, there can coexist a void and a sense of division within your being. This is because each part of your being needs its own special care, and not having it will cause each part of your being to be in disagreement with each other. I previously mentioned how I felt at times as if there were two of me with different perspectives constantly at war with one another. This feeling was due to the misalignment and disagreements taking place within my being. The only way to fix

YOU is to first have knowledge of your composition and the care you require.

The following chapters of this book are loaded with knowledge of your spirit, soul, and body.

Please take a few minutes to contemplate the images provided on the next page before we embark on a journey to self-discovery. As you read through the pages of this book, be mindful of each part of your being. This will help you identify the areas of need. Having knowledge of each part is equally important in order to obtain wholeness.

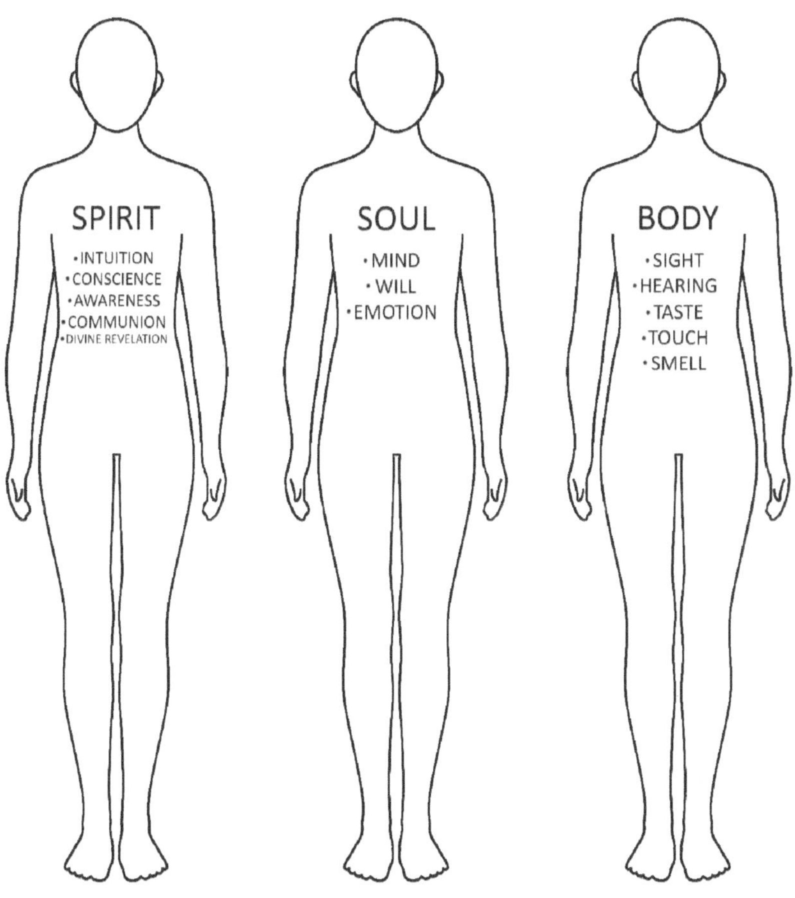

SPIRIT
•INTUITION
•CONSCIENCE
•AWARENESS
•COMMUNION
•DIVINE REVELATION
SOUL
•MIND
•WILL
•EMOTION
BODY
•SIGHT
•HEARING
•TASTE
•TOUCH
•SMELL

CHAPTER 2

The Spirit

(Part 1 of Your Being)

The spirit (conscience) of man is the lamp of the Lord,
Searching and examining all the innermost parts of his being.

—Prov. 20:27 (AMP)

Your spirit is the GPS that will help you navigate this earthly journey called life; it is the bridge that connects you to Divinity in the celestial realm. The word *Divinity* is indicative of Deity—Godhead, the Creator of heaven and earth and all that is in it.

Your spirit is breath, is intuitive, has a conscience, and has the ability to have spiritual communion with God and receive divine revelation and instruction from God. This part of your being is the purest and truest when it has been regenerated and maintains continual communion with God. It is also the most neglected part of one's being due to a lack of awareness and knowledge on how to care for it.

A person's spirit can find itself in different conditions or states. For instance, your spirit can be regenerated, dormant, or fallen. The best and highest state is "regenerated"—this is when a person's spirit has been spiritually renovated and has had a spiritual rebirth or spiritual revival. God is Spirit, and it is through the Spirit that God connects with man and man with God. In the regeneration process, man acquires awareness of the spiritual realm and becomes filled with the Spirit of God, also known as the Holy Spirit. Once "regenerated," your spirit and the Holy Spirit will share residency. The Holy Spirit is now dwelling on the inside of you. This is a great privilege and a gift from God to His children to help us navigate and succeed on this earthly journey.

Though all humans are spirit, not all humans have the Holy Spirit dwelling inside of them. Those that have not experienced "regeneration" have a dormant spirit—for better understanding, a spirit that is asleep or without awareness of God. A person whose spirit is asleep will use their reasoning or problem-solving skills to navigate life. Then, there are those who have experienced regeneration but did not continue cultivating a relationship with God and slowly revert to their old ways, causing them to have a fallen spirit. Both fall into the same category of mundane living, never experiencing the fullness of life or knowing the purpose of their existence.

Experiencing the regeneration of your spirit and cultivating a close relationship with God will change the whole dynamic of your inner man. Once your spirit is regenerated, it becomes empowered and positioned to receive divine revelation, instruction from God, and the ability to transmit and influence the other parts of your being, causing them to experience permanent transformation in accordance to God's perfect will.

It is possible that a regenerated spirit be depleted and become a fallen spirit if it loses its communion with God. Having daily communion with God is vital to the health of your spirit and imperative for the ongoing process of receiving, transmitting, and transforming. Hence, this is the process that will gradually mold you into the person God created you to be and to function in the fullness of your purpose and calling.

CHAPTER 3

The Soul

(Part 2 of Your Being)

*And the Lord God formed man of the dust of the
ground, and breathed into his nostrils the breath
of life; and man became a living soul.*

—Gen. 2:7 (KJV)

The soul is the seat of the mind, will, and emotions and is intertwined with the heart of man.

The soul is the part of man where difficulties lie and conflicts are present. It is the most perplexing part of one's being. Life experiences are reflected in the soul whether good or bad. Traumas, heartbreaks … all these things are stored in the soul of a man, leaving lifelong impressions.

The soul is living and in constant development. It is always in the process of becoming and is constantly being influenced by ideologies, systems, people, beliefs, cultures, and the many things of this world.

The soul is in constant battle, the battle of being saved or lost. The human soul is immortal and is destined to live in heaven or hell for eternity. The battle of the soul begins the moment we are born into this world. Unfortunately, we are not born with the foreknowledge of the battle or insight on how to save our own souls. It is with the guidance of the Holy Spirit and through the Word of God, we acquire the understanding and knowledge that will save our souls.

The Scripture says,

> ***That if you confess with your mouth the Lord Jesus and believe in your heart that God has raised Him from the dead, you will be saved. For with the heart one believes unto righteousness, and with the mouth, confession is made unto salvation. (Rom. 10:9 NKJV)***

Confessing and believing in your heart is your pass to salvation. Salvation guarantees an afterlife in eternity with God. The salvation of the soul belongs to Jesus Christ; the nurturing, care, and upkeep of the soul are your responsibility.

It is important to understand the needs of the soul for proper development and keeping it in a healthy state. The soul is at its best when it receives revelation from God and not information from the world. The Spirit of God reveals to your spirit; your spirit then transmits what's been revealed to your soul. Revelation is the knowledge of God being disclosed to humanity. This knowledge cannot be researched; it must be revealed by spiritual means versus natural information that can be researched and obtained by earthly means.

Nonetheless, the Spirit of God is not the only one influencing the soul. Your soul can also be influenced by the heart and one's carnal being. In the next chapter, you will learn about your body, a.k.a. your carnal being. Furthermore, I will also elaborate on the effect trauma has on the soul and the deep connection between the heart and soul.

CHAPTER 4

The Body

(Part 3 of Your Being)

***Watch and pray, lest you enter into temptation. The
spirit indeed is willing, but the flesh is weak.***

—Matt. 26:41 (NKJV)

The body, also known as the carnal being or the flesh, is the vehicle that will transport you through this earthly journey. The body represents an individual's carnality. It has five senses: sight, hearing, smell, touch, and taste. The senses make the body sensitive to earthly pleasures. As a result of its sensitivity, the body can easily be tempted; hence, it is the weakest part of an individual's being.

Because the body is weak and easily tempted, it must be placed under subjection. This is easier said than done, but with the help of the Holy Spirit, it is possible. Having dominion over the body will help you overcome unfruitful behaviors, desires, and appetites that can interrupt progress or even destroy life's purpose. On the other hand, the senses of the body also serve to protect, alert, and make aware.

Just like a camera captures an image that will serve as a memory of a moment in time, the body's senses are similar. They have the ability to capture memorable details such as a certain smell, taste, melody, texture, and color, hence bringing back memories. For instance, when I was in middle school, I had a friend who would use Salon Selectives hair spray to style his hair. I became very familiar with the smell so much that I associated the smell with him even to this day. In my case, being reminded of my friend brings back good childhood memories, but this is not always the case. It is also possible to have undesirable memories. Memories are life experiences stored in your soul and can arise without notice, hence provoking all kinds of emotions.

Furthermore, the physical body will thrive provided that it is given a healthy lifestyle. The body has needs such as eating, sleeping, having intimacy, etc. These are all valid needs and should be met with care and diligence. Additionally, prayer, fasting, daily exercise, and meditating on the Word of God are all good practices that will further add to the health of the body. Keep in mind that you will have one body for this journey, only one body; therefore, take good care of it!

CHAPTER 5

Three in One

*But let patience have its perfect work, that you may
be perfect and complete, lacking nothing.*

—James 1:4 (NKJV)

Each part of your being is special and unique; therefore, each part will need your undivided attention and its unique care and proper nutrition. However, the intent here is to have all three parts communicate in perfect harmony and be unified. Unfortunately, anything can interrupt harmony and take you off balance—a stressful day, a disagreement or argument, physical and emotional pain, or an unexpected life event. As you become more and more familiar with each part of your being, you will be able to identify any misalignments. Whenever you feel you have lost your balance, implementing basic practices will help you recover harmony of your being and regain your balance.

Remember the objective is to achieve an adequate order of performance that creates harmony. Your spirit should be the governing part since it is the truest part of your being and the connecting bridge to God. A healthy regenerated spirit leads under the guidance of the Holy Spirit. Since your soul is always in a becoming state. The soul needs daily renewal through the Word of God; therefore, its highest performance happens when it follows your spirit and not your flesh. Lastly, your body's highest performance occurs when it is kept healthy by exercise, good food, and remains submitted to the desires of your spirit.

To acquire an adequate order of performance will require you to be intentional in your doings. Implementing godly practices into your daily routine will undoubtedly start an organic flow of communication among your three-part being producing oneness and wholeness within you.

This may be easier said than done, but it is not impossible. The process of becoming anything good in life will require sacrifice and will have moments of highs and lows. Do not be discouraged if you suddenly take a dip and feel as if nothing is happening; something is always happening. Change starts on the inside before you see it on the outside. Lows are part of the process, and transformation occurs gradually just like that of a caterpillar turning into a beautiful butterfly, and once transformed, a butterfly will never be a caterpillar again. Have patience through the process and soon you will grow into a beautiful never-seen version of you.

Brokenness vs. wholeness. Both terms can be associated pretty much to anything, for instance, a broken glass, house, marriage, heart, etc. In this case, it's the human composite that we want to address. When any one part of your being is fragmented, your whole being is affected. Brokenness causes a vessel to become weak, and if left broken for a long period, chances are it will shatter or fall apart. The word "broken" in the English language is used to describe something that is not functioning properly. The same goes for a person who has a broken being, they are hindered from experiencing the fullness of a purpose-filled life. Wholeness is the absolute opposite of brokenness; it's the result of having your three-part being in oneness. Having wholeness points to a person that is complete in one piece, unbroken, undamaged, and undivided. As a consequence, they acquire better life results and have a stronger foundation. A person walking in wholeness is powerful because with wholeness comes internal strength, balance, mental clarity, the fullness of peace and joy, and the ability to remain focused and purpose-driven no matter the situation.

While intentionality, effort, and good work are your responsibility, the equation is not complete without the help of God Almighty! Wholeness is supernatural. It is produced by the combination of your diligence and your ongoing relationship with God. It is the product of the whole you becoming one with the One and the evidence of God's divine power at work in your life.

I know being broken is sorrowful. I was broken and was in a very dark place for most of my life. I also know that becoming whole is a choice. I willfully chose to embark on a journey to wholeness. In the beginning, I did a lot of reflecting and experienced much sadness, pain, and tears from past memories. Honestly, I thought I would never get better. As I took steps and drew closer to God, He became more and more real. He then met me in that very dark place. I soon began to see streaks of light coming through the darkness and a feeling of relief started settling within as the peace and love of God embraced me. These moments gave me the strength to continue taking forward steps, some days large, some days small. As I moved further into the journey, the sadness lifted, and the light shined brighter and brighter. I began having some of the most beautiful and, may I say, supernatural experiences with God that I would have never imagined. I was able to forgive genuinely—this was a first for me. I had held on to unforgiveness as if I was hurting the people that hurt me, not knowing this was only deteriorating my being. In essence, I was giving my offenders the ongoing power to harm my very spirit, soul, and body by keeping the memories alive. Gradually, I gained strength and experienced a love like no other—the love of God that is able to wipe away all the sorrow, heal and make you whole.

In all sincerity, trust the process, and give yourself permission to love, laugh, heal, and simply be happy with your true self. Always celebrate the small victories as you would the big ones; every victory matters!

Next, you will see examples of basic practices and nutrients that promote health and growth for your being and will help you on your journey to wholeness. Foremost, always remind yourself to embrace the challenges and enjoy the journey!

Basic Practices to a Better and Wholesome You

Get knowledge

Knowledge is power. You need revelatory transformative knowledge that is able to renew your mind and save your soul. Such knowledge is found in the Word of God. Set time aside each morning to read your Bible and pray. If you are a new believer in Christ and have not been introduced to the Holy Scriptures, I recommend you start by reading the four Gospels (Matthew, Mark, Luke, and John). Also find a version of the Bible that best suits your understanding.

Listen to testimonies

Hearing testimonies of faith-filled believers who, by the grace of God, have overcome life challenges will deposit faith into your being, and the hope and strength to believe you will overcome your challenges as well. Rest assured that if God did it for them, He will also do it for you. Testimonies have the power to stir up the spiritual realm and provoke God to do it again! Godly testimonies can be heard on social media, YouTube, and Spotify. There are also many good books written on this subject such as this one.

Create a safe environment

The places you visit and the people you associate yourself with matter. Create a circle of people that love, respect, and encourage your growth. Make friends with admirable faith-filled people who can give you good godly counsel and pray for and with you. After all, we all need—at the very least—one good friend!

Most importantly work on your faith

If you currently have little faith or no faith, not to worry, faith grows with continual exercise. Hearing the Word of God continually will help grow your faith. The Bible is not a book written to merely enhance your intellect or for entertainment. It is a spiritual book that reveals spiritual truths, in turn, strengthening and transforming your inner being. Faith is the key ingredient to overcoming impossibilities.

Nutrients That Will Promote Health and Growth for Your Being

First, identify which part of your being is suffering from malnutrition. Once identified, go to the list provided below, and select one nutrient specific to that part while making sure not to neglect any other part. If all three parts are in a state of malnutrition, select one nutrient specific to each part of your being, and incorporate them into your daily routine along with some of the basic practices discussed previously.

Nutrients for the spirit

- **Prayer.** Set a time to converse with God to express your thoughts and hardships.
- **Worship and praise.** Sing songs to God, and tell Him how great He is.
- **Make positive declarations.** Select several scriptures that resonate with you, and use them to make positive declarations over your life. For example, Philippians 4:13 says, "I can do all things through Christ who strengthens me." Take this scripture, and repeat it as often as possible until you believe it.
- **Express gratitude**. Remain in a state of thanksgiving and thank God for all He has done in your life and all the new things He is currently doing. Reflect on the goodness of God. Embrace the lessons and victories.

Nutrients for the soul

- **Read/study/meditate on the Scriptures**. Meditate on what you read, let the Word of God saturate your mind, and purify your thoughts (heart).

- **Fellowship.** Spend time with people who encourage and uplift you. People with godly wisdom that can provide you with sound counsel.
- **Give back.** Help someone in need. Serve in your church, do volunteer work and acts of kindness for those in need.
- **Enjoyment.** Take time to enjoy the things you like whether alone or with family and friends.

Nutrients for the body

- **Rest**. Designate at least one full day out of the week to completely relax and let go.
- Sleep seven to nine hours per day.
- Exercise/stretch.
- Hydrate.
- Cut down sugars and caffeine.
- Select wholesome foods instead of processed foods.
- Take breathing breaks.
- Take cold showers.

Keep in mind that any time you start something new or venture off into the unknown, it is inevitable to feel scared, unbalanced, anxious, or even overwhelmed. These feelings can make you want to give up and revert to your comfort zone, but it is all part of the process.

Don't be afraid of breaking up with the familiar. It's uncomfortable, I know! But understand your best is not in the familiar. Prepare to declutter your life to let go of old customs, people, places, and things. At times, you will resist the new things simply because you have found comfort in the old ways of doing things, but if you are serious about becoming the best YOU, you must be fully committed to the process and understand that the old ways will only keep you bound to your past. Staying consistent with forward motion will create inevitable personal growth and make the way for a better YOU each day.

Following is a list of conditions a person can experience during the process of transformation as one is leaving the old and entering the new. I have also formulated sample scenarios to demonstrate how one can become resistant to change and sabotage personal growth. Thankfully, you can stop this by implementing some of the intervention strategies I have provided for you below.

Conditions you may experience throughout your journey

When you experience the following, it's an indicator that your spirit is lacking nutrition:

- **Doubt.** An indicator that you have little faith for the challenge you are facing or have incomplete faith—faith for some things but not for others. In this case, you have to work on increasing your faith. Faith is increased by hearing the Word of God. The Word of God will help you change your perspective, and through faith-filled thinking, you will build a strong mental foundation that will push out doubt.

- **Fear**. The opposer of your faith. Fear is also the absence of love. You must believe in your heart that Jesus loves you and He is for you and not against you. No matter how lonely this walk may feel or how troublesome life may get, you must always draw close to Him—the Author and Finisher of your faith. Meditating on scriptures that reveal God's unending and unconditional love will help to cast out all fear from your being.

- **Low energy.** When you encounter challenges and hardships, you can feel depleted. To regain your strength, spend time in God's presence reading, praying, and listening to worship music—all these things will refresh and recharge your spirit. In addition, it is very important to remove all distractions and get physical rest as this is a mandate from God and is very necessary to regain focus and clarity.

- **Lack of direction or confusion.** Confusion is not orchestrated by God. A word from God will move you in the right direction and will always give you peace. Pray for direction, and follow through with reading the scriptures. The Word of God will highlight the path you should take.

- **Overpowered by cravings and urges.** When your spirit is empty or has become exhausted, your body will try to fill the void with pleasures. To recover control, prepare to fast for several days (at least three days) by abstaining from certain foods, social media, TV, electronic devices, and all distractions. Replace your regular meals with liquids, vegetables, or fruits. During your fast, you must have some quiet time to read the scriptures, pray, praise, worship, and be still. This will help your natural body detox while strengthening your spirit. Being in stillness will allow you to hear from God and regain dominion over your being.

- **Feeling of boredom or emptiness.** You are not doing enough meaningful things. Volunteer, serve, and do acts of kindness for people who need it. This will give you a sense of purpose and fulfillment.

- **Depression, anxiety, inability to rest.** It is always good to talk and pray with God-fearing and trustworthy authorities like pastors, mentors, and friends. If the depression or anxiety is being caused by past trauma, consider visiting a certified Christian therapist knowledgeable in the process of healing and deliverance of the soul. Most importantly, trust God, rest in His presence, and know that only He can lift your burdens.

Example Scenarios #1—Resistance

An opportunity has opened within your company. You have been hoping for a promotion. The opening is for the position you desire. Without hesitation, you immediately access the application online and begin filling it out. Midway, a doubtful thought creeps into your mind that says, "I don't think I meet the requirements." After that one thought, a flow of similar thoughts raids your mind, so much so that your insecurities take over and fully convince you that you do not qualify for the job. Immediately you stop your pursuit and do not submit the application.

What is happening here? The negative thoughts are being drawn out from your soul where lifelong experiences, trauma, and beliefs are stored. Whether negative or positive, your thoughts have the ability to influence your decisions and impact the future outcome of a thing.

This scenario reveals the need to renew the mind to replace old beliefs with sound truths. Beware, unresolved trauma leaves behind residue and creates triggers that can continually show up without notice. Thankfully, the Word of God is the ultimate Truth; it is able to heal the soul, renew the mind, and oppose the thoughts that are resisting change.

Example Scenarios #2—Resistance

Your usual decompressing habits after work are having dinner while watching your favorite TV show and scrolling on social media. Recently, you decided on a workout plan that includes a low-calorie diet, attending the gym after work, and going to sleep earlier than usual. On the third day, you are feeling extremely hungry, sore, and tired and would much rather be home engaging in your old routine. Clearly your BODY, a.k.a. carnal being or flesh, is uncomfortable and is not welcoming changes. If you yield to your body, it is more than likely you will revert to your old ways. Your mind has to conquer this moment. You have set a workout goal. In order to accomplish the goal, you must push forward with your mind and not your feelings. Try taking a quick cold shower before your workout. This can help increase alertness, energy levels, and endurance. Also, prepare your body throughout the day by eating foods that promote energy, and make sure to drink enough water to keep your body hydrated. Most importantly, make sure to start your morning with prayer. Prayer energizes your entire being and sets a good foundation for the rest of your day.

Having the awareness of which part of your being is resilient to change will help you put together an action plan to build and help your being transition into the new.

These are simplified but valid scenarios to show how your being can sabotage growth and resist change, but keep in mind there are different levels of resistance you will encounter when trying to become the best version of YOU. Rule of thumb: anything that sabotages your growth or is resilient to change must be dealt with consistently until you have conquered it.

CHAPTER 6

Dive into the Depth of Your Soul

For those who live according to the flesh set their minds on the things of the flesh, but those who live according to the Spirit, the things of the Spirit. For to be carnally minded is death, but to be spiritually minded is life and peace.

—Rom. 8:5–6 (NKJV)

And be renewed in the spirit of your mind.

—Eph. 4:23 (NKJV)

The soul is the most perplexing part of one's being and concurrently the most important one.

From the time of birth, we enter into an unseen battle, the battle of and for the soul. The soul is the most valuable part of one's being, that is why it is so sought after both by heaven and hell. The soul is a vitality, the immortal part of man. The condition of the soul determines where man will live for eternity. This battle will be with us for a lifetime. You are the only one that can end the battle by choosing who you will serve, God or the world.

This chapter will break down the different functions, conflicts, and battles in one's soul.

The mind, will, and emotions of a human being are interconnected and are located within the soul, and they affect each other like a ripple effect. When your mind produces a thought, that thought produces an emotion, and these thoughts and emotions will have influence on your will and play a big role in decision-making.

Mental health issues, traumas, and heartbreaks are some of the things that affect the health of the soul greatly. The soul can also be oppressed and influenced by demonic spirits. In this case, deliverance is necessary prior to and throughout the healing process.

Let us explore the three parts of the soul (mind, will, and emotions), its functions, and what happens to the soul when it is wounded.

The mind is spirit and intellect. It is a place of imagination, understanding, and mental vigor. The mind is the dominant part of your soul, but your mind is greatly influenced by the thoughts of one's heart, in turn affecting the entire soul.

When dealing with the mind, you MUST be intentional. The mind has a tendency of drifting off into its own adventures of thoughts. Not all thoughts are worth entertaining. Thoughts cause emotions; therefore, thoughts can create your happiness or sadness and can give you courage or fears. Some thoughts are wildly imaginative; others are extremely over-reactive. Thoughts are constantly being formulated in your mind. By having awareness of your thoughts, you can take control of all negative thoughts before they take control of you.

The mind is so powerful, it can bypass physical disabilities. There are people with physical impairments that are able to do more than those with perfectly healthy bodies. Why is this? Well, it is because freedom starts in the spirit of your mind, not in your physical body. Your mind sets the limitations or possibilities according to your beliefs and thought patterns.

Everything begins with a thought! If you are not intentional with your thoughts, the systems and the many ideologies of this world will take residency in your mind and will mold your life according to the world's standards. On the other hand, if you purposely start to deposit spiritual truths into your mind, your mind will be renewed, and your thoughts will be according to God's thoughts, and He will be the architect of your life.

The mind requires what it requires, and that is nonetheless spiritual truth! When you feed the mind spiritual truth, transformation is inevitable because the spirit of your mind undergoes a spiritual renovation. The process of renewal happens when negative thoughts are replaced with spiritual truths. When spiritual truths start to take residency in your mind, the old thoughts are evicted, making the spiritual truths your reality. When the Word of God (spiritual truth) is engrafted in your mind, it does not only change your reality, but it is also able to save your soul.

Before I became a Christian, I tried many methods to better my life, but I never acquired true change, and somehow I always felt empty and discouraged. I tried different religions, read self-help books, tried detox methods, and even participated in several seminars and retreats, but nothing helped! The one thing I am thankful for is that I never stopped searching for answers because the continual searching and desire to become better eventually led me to the Truth … just like the scriptures say, "seek and you shall find." I found the Truth, and it set me free.

The will expresses one's determination, inclination, choices, and desires.

The will is strong and likes to take action based on what it wills to do. The human will is influenced by desires, beliefs, thoughts, and emotions. There are times we have the knowledge to do what is right, but we desire to do otherwise. The will does not always take action on what it knows; it also takes action based on feelings and desires. The mind and the emotions serve as influencers of the will, but the highest influence comes from one's spirit. When your spirit is regenerated and led by the Holy Spirit of God, it is easy to submit your will to God. You are making willful decisions daily. These decisions are molding your future, and the healthier your soul, the better the outcome.

The emotions are formed according to one's mental perception of things. Thoughts, memories, beliefs, and your five senses are some of the factors that contribute to your emotions. Having uncontrolled emotions is one of the leading causes of errors; hence, an emotional person is easily manipulated, enticed, or triggered. Emotions are good so long as they are expressed and handled with care. You don't want to become numb to the world, and you also don't want to become an emotional roller coaster. Self-control and balance is the key here!

A Wounded Soul

The soul is wounded when a person suffers any type of trauma. Wounds in the soul cause imbalances. These imbalances will reflect in your everyday life. Picture a wounded soldier on a battlefield: he doesn't lose his soldier status, but he does lose strength and becomes limited in the battle. That's exactly what happens when the soul gets wounded. You are not functioning to the fullness of your capacity.

There is no big or little trauma. Trauma to the soul can happen to anyone. As a matter of fact, everyone at some point will go through some type of event that will affect their soul. The loss of a loved one, abandonment, offenses, betrayal, abuse, a shock or a scare, an accident, etc. These are just some events that can be traumatic to the soul. Some people experience one, while others may experience a sequence of events throughout the course of their lives. Nonetheless, whether one or many, trauma is trauma and can cause great damage to the soul.

In fact, the world is full of wounded souls; many put all their efforts into gains but walk around with an immense internal void. The truth is that no matter the accomplishments or material gains a person has, they will never experience the fullness of life if their soul is damaged. The wounds of the soul yearn to be healed; no one enjoys being broken, full of sorrow, and pain. While wounds hold the soul captive, healing liberates the soul. Being healed does not necessarily mean the traumatic experience is removed from your memory bank; what it means is that the wound is no longer bleeding. A healed person can live freely, love without measure, and laugh loudly because the burden has been lifted.

Further in the book, we will explore the negative effects and dangers of trauma on the soul.

CHAPTER 7

Meet the Heart

Keep your heart with all diligence, For
out of it spring the issues of life.

—Prov. 4:23 (NKJV)

Blessed are the pure in heart, For they shall see God.

—Matt. 5:8 (NKJV)

The heart is the center of man and also an access point to the soul. The heart has thoughts, feelings, desires, intellect, understanding, and a will. The heart is said to be deceitful above all things and desperately wicked, but on a separate note, a wholesome heart is the life and health of your being and is also known as the international symbol of love. The heart is controversial in character and its intentions questionable at times. I have found there is more to the heart than we know…

Why is the heart said to be deceitful?

Every human is born in iniquity, conceived in sin, and born with a sinful heart. Sin comes from the earth, not from heaven. Therefore, the heart of man is earthbound; it is the organ that keeps the natural body moving, and the part of man that connects with earthly feelings. For this very reason, we must constantly check our hearts and do our best to purify them from earthly contaminants. The heart, like the soul, can be transformed. Though the human heart's inclination is earthly, it is possible to align one's heart to God's heart by yielding your will to His will like King David, who was a man after God's own heart and yielded his own will to do God's will.

Upon conception, there are genetics transferred on to us, and these genetics are inclusive of God's image and likeness and the iniquity of our parents and past generations. Humans harbor both the good and the bad in their being.

Let's analyze the early years of childhood. Once a child is able to crawl or walk, they will go right past the toys and grab ahold of the electrical outlet. It's the harmful things that pique their curiosity, and this is due to the iniquity present in their DNA. As a parent, you will spend a great portion of your time teaching your child through constant correction. Just like our Heavenly Father who has given us His Word to help us learn and grow in righteousness. The Word of God corrects and makes straight those things that somehow through the course of life have been made crooked. It has the power to draw out the iniquity from the heart, change your perspective, and give you the instructions needed for a better life.

Through the reading of the Word of God along with a continual relationship with God, your heart will be healed, purified, filled with faith, and made whole. As the Word of God washes your inner being, the desire to evolve and do better is inevitable. When the Word of God is engrafted into your heart, you will know true love, and your heart will beat to a different rhythm, and before you know it, your life is being transformed.

Most importantly, you should know that the heart and soul are intertwined; they have the deepest of connections. The heart shares its thoughts, feelings, and desires with the soul. For this very reason, anything that affects your heart will also affect your soul. The heart, like the soul, must be cared for and kept with diligence because these two centers determine the course of your life. The heart will determine the condition of your earthly life, and the state of your soul will determine your eternal residency. Keep in mind there are only two places where a man can live for eternity; heaven or hell.

The Gatekeeper of Your Heart

And the peace of God, which surpasses all understanding, will guard your hearts and minds through Christ Jesus.

—Phil. 4:7 (NKJV)

Your heart is very much involved in the formation of your reality and the salvation of your soul. I would say it's valuable and merits safety.

The heart needs a gatekeeper, someone who is not enticed by earthly things, who will not negotiate the key to your heart, and who is solely vested in the well-being of your heart and soul. Jesus Christ is the only one who fits the description. He holds an exclusive key, the key that opens doors that no person can close and closes doors that no person can open. This key no one has! When you genuinely love God with all your heart and surrender control to Him, He will fill you with His love, removing your need to be validated or settle for false love. His love is pure and truly fulfilling like no other. Just as He closes the door to unfruitful things that will harm your heart, He will open the door at the right time for the perfect love!

God is undoubtedly the best gatekeeper of the heart; alongside Him, you also have the obligation to exercise safety over your heart. Through God's Holy Spirit, the Word, and continual communion with Him, you will be able to discern what are harmful and unhealthy situations for your heart. The Holy Spirit of God is great at nudging you, making you aware of trouble—at times He will even reroute you without notice.

A heart vested in God searches for godly things and does not need validation from the world. It knows what it wants and finds it in God. Once you have experienced the love of God and His goodness, you willfully will have the desire to remove toxic people, places, and things from your life.

Boundaries Are Necessary

Setting boundaries is extremely important. For instance, when a new person comes into my life, I require time to learn about the person. I am never too careful and always seek God to know if this is a purposeful relationship sent by Him. People can come into your life with the sole intention of fulfilling their own agendas. Therefore, you cannot call just anyone your friend or assume they are trustworthy. These titles must be earned, and earning them takes time.

Pay attention to people's actions and behaviors but most of all to the conversation. The words that come out of a person's mouth say a lot about them and their intentions. Look for things in common, core values, and morals. If you have fundamental differences, this is an indication there is no substance to build on. For instance, I reunited with an old schoolmate during a church event. I had not seen this person for over twenty years. Though we shared the same religious beliefs, after some time, it was obvious that we did not have the same core values and had many fundamental differences. Eventually, the relationship ended because there was nothing to build on.

This approach keeps my circle small, brings me success, and minimizes heartbreaks and troubles. I keep it very simple. If it does not align with God's Word and purpose for my life, there is no room for it in my heart. I encourage you to do the same … set boundaries that work for you.

Double-Mindedness Is a Condition of the Heart

He is a double-minded man, unstable in all his ways.

—James 1:8 (NKJV)

*Draw near to God and He will draw near
to you. Cleanse your hands, you sinners; and
purify your hearts, you double-minded.*

—James 4:8 (NKJV)

Being double-minded is a condition of the heart. A double-minded person is torn between feelings and understanding. This happens when the feelings in the heart oppose the knowledge of the heart. This disagreement causes vacillation (wavering) also known as being "two-spirited." Decision-making becomes difficult when you know the right thing to do but are completely overtaken by what you feel in your heart. It's two opposites at war with equal strength… the question is, Who will win this tug-of-war?

If it enters your heart, it has access to your being. When your heart is set on something, you will be overtaken with the desire to have it. The heart can easily convince the mind to have what it wants, whether it's good or bad. The heart is not to be trusted when it comes to making decisions because it moves on feelings. Protecting your heart is extremely important, because the things that enter your heart are able to affect the outcome of your entire life.

For example, when people get married, they experience love with their hearts (feelings), but if these feelings are not backed up by a grounded decision, one that will prevail over feelings, the relationship will not last very long. Feelings can change for whatever reason(s), and when they do, people get discouraged and in most cases even seek divorce. Relationships should be founded on a higher Truth, not feelings. Feelings fluctuate and have many variables. Lasting love is a decision to love past the butterflies.

What are the effects of double-mindedness?

A person with a "double mind" is indecisive, expresses divided loyalty, may be influenced by many beliefs, is unstable, has sinful tendencies, tends to run cold on some days and hot on others, like a yo-yo or seesaw they have many ups and downs, and may even disagree with self. This state of mind is depleting, can feel tormenting, withholds progress, and can escalate into serious mental health issues. The Bible advises against double-mindedness and emphasizes we are to be of one mind and one spirit.

When making decisions, I recommend you do the necessary research to weigh out your options, then go for it or drop it and move on. If adjustments are needed, make them along the way, but do not stay in a state of indecisiveness because you will accomplish nothing.

Get your mind right!

The solution to a "double mind" requires turning away from sin, purifying the heart, and renewing your mind through the Word of God. When your mind is renewed by the Word of God, your old ways of thinking are flushed out, and the new godly knowledge sets in and becomes your new way of thinking. A renewed mind is grounded and sustained by the Word of God.

Yes, turn away from "sin." Please don't feel offended we have all missed the mark. Sin is the cause of knowing the right thing to do and not doing it. I get it! It is easier said than done but not impossible. Look around, the world is full of people that have overcome huge obstacles and those that are continually overcoming them. You can too! Be intentional, practice the good and godly ways, and you will produce better results in everything you do.

Watch out for these things!

Although courage lies in the heart, the heart is also susceptible in nature. Things like betrayal, disappointment, abandonment, offense, and even the loss of a loved one can act as potential hazards to the heart. In some instances, you will be able to take measures to protect your heart; in others, it will take you by surprise—causing a heartbreak. A heartbreak can be hard to overcome, but staying in a state of brokenness can cause greater dangers like one of a hardened heart. This is a condition in which the heart becomes emotionally and spiritually numbed. A numbed heart can cause a person to live in continual sin, lose passion for life, and even lose their soul.

Surely, the intentions and thoughts of a damaged heart are questionable. Therefore, keep your heart by forgiving quickly; repenting genuinely; and do not allow offenses, rejections, perversion, or negative feelings or thoughts to take residency in your heart. Fill your heart with gratitude, love, compassion, kindness, and goodwill as there is reciprocity and fulfillment in this. Most importantly, a grounded faith and strong foundation in the Word of God will heal and restore health back to your heart and soul. A trustworthy heart is one that is healed, pure, and fully submitted to God.

CHAPTER 8

Trauma and the Soul

All of Jacob's children came to comfort him,
but he refused to be comforted. "No," he
said, "I will go to my grave, mourning for
my son." So Jacob kept on grieving.

—Gen. 37:35 (CEV)

Jacob is deceived to believe that his son Joseph has died, and immediately he goes into shock. An immense feeling of despair consumes Jacob, and for approximately thirteen years, Jacob grieves for his son Joseph. Like Jacob, many people go through painful events that leave them broken and stuck in a traumatic state.

> *² She sent a message to Elijah: "You killed my prophets. Now I'm going to kill you! I pray that the gods will punish me even more severely if I don't do it by this time tomorrow."*
> *³ Elijah was afraid when he got her message, and he ran to the town of Beersheba in Judah. He left his servant there,*
> *⁴ then walked another whole day into the desert. Finally, he came to a large bush and sat down in its shade. He begged the Lord, "I've had enough. Just let me die! I'm no better off than my ancestors." (1 Kings 19:2–4 CEV)*

31

This is Elijah's mood after overcoming a battle against 450 prophets of Baal. Shortly after the battle, he receives a message from Jezebel, the queen of Israel, saying she is coming after his life, and when Elijah hears this, he feels absolute terror. You would think this evident warrior would respond with confidence and say to her "Bring it on!" But no, instead of being fearless, he is fearful even after his success in executing the 450 prophets of Baal. The truth is, not all victories are worthy of celebration. The journey to victory can be full of hardships, challenges, and pain as well as being long and strenuous.

Like a divorce, court cases, immigration process, overcoming addiction, abuse, and the list goes on. There are battles that can cause trauma to the soul even on the way to victory.

We don't plan for traumatic events; they just show up. For instance, on a very snowy night, my daughter would be arriving at the Denver airport. And I was scheduled to pick her up. On my way to the airport, I was caught in a snowstorm. I was driving my daughter's car, and, of course, it had no windshield washer fluid which is helpful for visibility during a snowstorm. As I drove, I realized my visibility was less and less; everything was white, the roads, cars—everything, just everything! I went into total panic and did everything possible to gain visibility so I could find my way off the highway. I even resorted to putting my head out the window, but nothing worked—it just made it worse. Now my glasses were wet, and I really could not see. I continued on the path, slowly following the brightness of the taillights of the vehicles traveling in front of me, and finally arrived at the airport safely by the grace of God. Though I arrived in one piece and did not cause any accidents on the road, truthfully and internally, I did not feel safe at all! Something happened to me that day. When I finally parked the car and realized I was at the Denver airport. I was relieved but at the same time in a state of panic; in fact, I was not able to drive back home. My daughter, who had just gotten off a long tiresome flight, had to drive us home. Honestly, I think I was willing to sleep on the airport floor that night, but there was no way I was getting behind the wheel again. As you can imagine, the drive back home was long, thankfully we made it home safe. For the rest of the night, I remained in a state of thanksgiving; all I could do was thank God for the outcome despite the inclement weather conditions. As the days went by, I thought nothing of it and just put it behind me, so I thought.

For the next year, any time I was on a highway I would randomly get panic attacks, my palms would break into a sweat, and my heart would begin to race for no evident reason. In order to avoid feeling this way, I purposely changed the settings on my GPS to navigate on "no highway." The more I brushed off the signs of a problem, thinking the feeling would go away, the worse the symptoms became.

It was evident the snowstorm event had a negative impact on me. I became frustrated and somewhat depressed. Maybe because I am not the type that likes to feel limited. I have spent a lifetime overcoming obstacles, and was determined to overcome this as well, but I must admit it was not that easy. The feeling was uncontrollable, and the anxiety and panic would just show up unannounced. Although I managed it, and no one noticed what I was going through, it was a horrible feeling, one I could not conform to. This thing and I were not about to become friends.

So I did what I know to do and sought God in prayer and fasting. During this time, God allowed me to see how the spirit of fear entered my being and settled in my soul on the day of the snowstorm. It was specifically the fear of death. At the time of the incident, my mother had recently passed, and I was still mourning her. The sorrow in my heart made my spirit weak and vulnerable. The spirit of fear found an access point into my soul because of my vulnerability, which in turn made the snowstorm incident a traumatic experience for me especially since the death of my mother was unexpected and was caused by an accidental fall.

The Bible teaches that fear is a spirit and not one given by God. It will enter slowly and whisper words of despair, and before you know it, it has taken over your thoughts, paralyzing your being and causing depression and severe anxiety as was happening to me.

So I became very intentional in strengthening my spirit. I specifically prayed against the spirit of fear and asked God to heal the damage it caused my soul. I took action to confront fear head-on. I weatherproofed my vehicle; next I purposely began to get on the highway during daylight. I went for short drives in the snow to regain my confidence, but most importantly, I continually made declarations against fear throughout the day. I repeated and repeated every scripture I could find against fear until it was embedded in my heart and mind. Eventually, healing took its course, and I gradually overcame the anxiety of driving on the highway. Had I ignored the signs and made permanent accommodations to calm the fear, I would have probably never driven on a highway again and most likely never would have made beautiful Colorado my home. That traumatic incident would have sabotaged all the great opportunities, friendships, and blessings this place has given me. Trauma stops progress and eats away at your blessings.

For Jacob, it was the loss of a son that kept him in bondage for approximately thirteen years, for Elijah a death threat that kept him in severe fear for approximately forty days/nights, and for me a snowstorm that kept me off highways for a little over one year. Oh! And let's not forget to mention a global pandemic like COVID-19 that turned the world upside-down in a span of two years and has left many traumatized and in fear. Anything can pose a threat and become a trauma to your soul. Big or little, the size of a trauma is not measured by the type of event; it's measured by the impact it causes an individual. Keep in mind that everyone processes differently and what may be traumatic to me may not be at all to you or vice versa, so don't take anything lightly. Know that any traumatic experience can leave you vulnerable and an access point to demonic spirits. Don't be passive when it comes to your soul.

Have you checked in with yourself lately? Is there an area where you stopped seeing progress? Are you easily triggered or have random panic attacks? Do you sabotage opportunities? Are you seeing destructive cycles, "the-same-of-the-same" in different places, with different faces but always similar situations? If this is you, it's time to strengthen your spirit and confront the things that are affecting your soul and life progress!

What is trauma?

The word *trauma* is frequently misinterpreted. Trauma is not to be measured by the severity or outcome of any incident. Trauma is a result of a negative experience that afflicts a person psychologically or physically; its effects linger for an extended period and in some cases for a lifetime. Living with prolonged sorrow is a result of trauma and will cause your spirit to become broken and weak. The negative effects of trauma can ramify into all areas of your body and life, causing further damage to your current and future life. For this very reason, processing and confronting negative experiences immediately are the wisest actions one can take to avoid trauma from taking permanent residency in your soul.

When trauma is present in the soul, it affects your mind, will, and emotions. It alters behavior, personality, and perspective due to the pain and deception attached to the experience. A person in a traumatic state can experience the following conditions but are not limited to; isolation, fears, phobias, illnesses, anxiety, addiction, depression, feeling incapable or at a disadvantage, feeling entrapped or restrained, not able to be your truest self, feeling perplexed or uncertain, not able to make good/clear decisions, memory loss, and having no recollection or having cloudy thoughts.

Many cognitive neuroscience studies confirm memory loss or isolation of memories due to a traumatic experience. While the memories may have been lost or clouded, the effect of an unresolved trauma can still be present for years to come. Studies also reveal that a great percentage of adults currently seeking therapy in the United States for mental health issues, addictions, anxiety, depression, etc. have unresolved childhood traumas that have ramified and intensified with time.

Physical trauma can turn into psychological trauma and vice versa. For example, an accident can cause physical trauma, but the impact of the accident can also stay lingering in the mind far past the healing of the physical body. The fear and anguish felt during the accident can now cause psychological trauma.

In the case of psychological trauma, the mind dwells on painful memories. This causes distress to the physical body which will, in turn, cause illness or disorders such as anxiety, heart problems, high blood pressure, eating disorders, depression, etc.

Pain is debilitating in both types of experience and may drive people to resort to coping mechanisms like alcohol, drugs, and quick fixes to defuse the pain, not knowing these types of coping mechanisms cause greater damage.

To say that you will never have a traumatic experience is unrealistic. The loss of a loved one can pose us trauma, and we all know death is inevitable. No one can be assured of a perfect life without troubles, but there is hope that when troubles come, there are healthy ways to overcome them. In fact, the Word of God confirms that everyone in the world will experience some type of tribulation(s), but if we put our eyes on Jesus, He will give us the grace and guidance to overcome the best way possible.

Jesus has promised us freedom, peace, healing, and restoration of the soul. His Word is a road map to a better life. Below are some scriptures to encourage and remind you that in Jesus, you are never alone.

Scriptures That Will Encourage You

> *These things I have spoken to you, that in Me you may have peace. In the world you will have tribulation; but be of good cheer, I have overcome the world. (John 16:33 NKJV)*

> *Lord, my God, I cried out to you for help, and you healed me. (Psalm 30:2 CEB)*

> *When I was really hurting, I prayed to the Lord. He answered my prayer, and took my worries away. (Psalm 118:5 CEV)*

> *Therefore if the Son makes you free, you shall be free indeed. (John 8:36 NKJV)*

The Lord is my shepherd; I shall not want. He makes me to lie down in green pastures; He leads me beside the still waters. He restores my soul; He leads me in the paths of righteousness For His name's sake. (Psalm 23:1–3 NKJV)

CHAPTER 9

Taking Back the Pieces

Jesus answered and said to her, "If you knew the gift of God, and who it is who says to you, 'Give Me a drink,' you would have asked Him, and He would have given you living water."

—**John 4:10 (NKJV)**

There is a beautiful story in the Bible about a Samaritan woman who meets her Savior at a well. This Samaritan woman has a history of misfortune and heartbreaks stemming from five failed marriages and the possibility of a barren womb. The culture and times were not very forgiving to divorced women, which means she was more than likely a social outcast, criticized by many and full of shame and suffering. For a very long time, I felt just like the woman at the well, brokenhearted, full of shame, and desperate for change. The same Jesus that went out of His way to meet the woman at the well with the intent of saving, healing, and transforming her is the same Jesus that met me in my living room one day.

That day I was praying as I usually do. A short time into my prayer, I felt like just sitting quietly in meditation. When Jesus walked into my living room, His presence was heavy in the room, and tears began rolling down my cheeks. Then a vision almost like a movie trailer was before me. It was a replay of my past. I saw many people, some holding in their hands pieces of my heart and soul. As I strolled down memory lane, I experienced mixed feelings. Some memories made me laugh, and others made me cry. It was apparent that some of the relationships revealed in the vision had a negative effect on me. If the truth be told, some were very troublesome. I learned that day that time passed, but the damage caused by those relationships had been with me all along. Any time you vest your heart, time, and energy into something, and for whatever reason, it does not work, you are left with disappointment, shame, and distrust, and all the brokenness is stored in your soul.

It was right then and there that I made a firm decision to take back every piece of my heart and soul, and I allowed God to enter those areas and heal every open wound. As I was on my knees, I mentioned every name of every person as I was seeing them in the vision. As I said their name, I also said, "I forgive you," and also asked for their forgiveness. Then I reached into each one of their hands and took back the pieces of my heart and soul. Toward the end of the vision, I felt a burden lifting off me. I knew the Holy Spirit of God was healing and delivering me. A sense of freedom and joy overtook me, and the tears kept rolling down my face, but this time it was tears of joy. I felt God pour His love over me, and I heard a small still voice in my spirit say, "Now, you can love again"**(Rom. 5:5 NKJV)**. Finally, all the work and obedience in my healing journey paid off. This is evidence that if you do your human part, God will do the miraculous **(Zech. 4:6 NKJV).**

> *⁵ Now hope does not disappoint, because the love of God has been poured out in our hearts by the Holy Spirit who was given to us. (ROM 5:5 NKJV)*

> *This is the word of the Lord to Zerubbabel: 'Not by might nor by power, but by My Spirit,' Says the Lord of hosts. (Zach 4:6 NKJV)*

Today, I can say with confidence that I am chosen and loved unconditionally despite the many mishaps in my life. I am a woman who has been saved, healed, and transformed by the glorious gift of God, the gift of living water. This gift is not only for me but for everyone who believes.

CHAPTER 10

Forgiveness Is a Must

*This is how I want you to conduct yourself in these matters.
If you enter your place of worship and, about to make an
offering, you suddenly remember a grudge a friend has
against you, abandon your offering, leave immediately,
go to this friend and make things right. Then and only
then, come back and work things out with God.*

—Matt. 5:24 (MSG)

From a very young age and throughout my whole life, there has been a very loud internal voice that is constantly saying "There is more." This voice has been the one to encourage me and pushed me to get up from every failure. It is the voice that kept me moving through depression and every hardship of my life. This voice led me on a journey of self-discovery. I was desperate to find out all about the whys. Why do bad things happen to me? Why can't I succeed at anything? Why am I a mess? Why such sadness and void in me? In conclusion, the list of whys was longer than my children's Christmas list. While I did not have answers for the whys, I did find that life's purpose is bigger than the whys I often questioned.

Forgiveness erased the whys and amplified, even more, the internal voice that kept saying "There is more!" The things that happened to me were not nearly as important as the courage and strength they produced in me.

Forgiveness played a big role in my healing journey. I started by forgiving every person that hurt me, every failure, every betrayal, and most importantly myself. The more I forgave, the freer I felt. I didn't realize that by not forgiving, I was holding myself hostage for the actions of others, empowering them to continue hurting me. I found the more I forgave, the clearer the path to purpose became. Then the whys stopped, and I started asking God to show me the way to more.

Unforgiveness is a toxin. The ramification will cause you physical and mental illnesses, delay your spiritual growth, and stop you from experiencing true love and the goodness of God. Worst of all, it endangers your soul and can cause you to lose your salvation. Is not the gospel about forgiveness? We all need forgiveness, and Jesus has given us just that! Therefore, you must learn to forgive others.

Once unforgiveness was out of my heart, God didn't hold back. He gave me a fresh filling of His Spirit, started pouring revelation into me, gave me the ability to press through in prayer, and provided me with wisdom and understanding. Now God is continually expanding my abilities to do and be more. When I stopped focusing on people's opinions, let go of all offenses, and placed my eyes on God, my thoughts became higher, and I understood that I must do everything unto God and not unto people. Trying to please people will leave you empty time and time again and will only distance you from God. In all you do, make sure to glorify God, and let God handle the people.

I can truly and with all confidence say I serve the God of more, my God has no equal, and there is no other god like Him. His purpose for your life is greater than you can imagine and greater than any pain we've suffered. He is the God that will turn every tear in your favor. I encourage you to keep your mind and eyes set on Jesus, and He will show you great things.

Practices You Can Put in Place to Help You with the Forgiveness Process

In Christ we are made free by his blood sacrifice. We have forgiveness of sins because of God's rich grace.

—Eph. 1:7 (ERV)

Let the above scripture marinate in your heart. The Father gave His only Son, Jesus, who is right standing and without sin, to die a gruesome death, one of bloodshed and crucifixion for the forgiveness of our sins. Would you not agree that forgiveness is crucial and without doubt a message and mandate from God to the world?

I understand forgiveness is hard, but knowing that forgiveness has great benefits for your being should make it easier to forgive. Don't dwell on past memories; just decide to forgive by taking action toward it. Forgiveness is a process and does not happen overnight. You must be diligent and intentional with your actions. That is why the first step is to ask God to give you the grace to forgive, then pray for the person who hurt you and declare blessing over them, and make declarations like "I forgive you [*say the person's name*]." Practice forgiveness by doing acts of kindness, for example, if the person is reachable and there is no conflict of interest, you may want to send a onetime letter with no return address simply to express your forgiveness.

For example,

> Dear (*name*),
>
> Hope this letter finds you well. I just want to let you know that your actions hurt me. I've started the healing process with the help of Jesus Christ and want you to know I have forgiven you. If I have ever hurt you in any way, please

find it in your heart to forgive me as well. I wish
you nothing but the best. God bless you.

This process is helpful for those that are looking to restore as
well as for those who need to forgive and let go.

CHAPTER 11

Faith to Heal

And suddenly, a woman who had a flow of blood for twelve years came from behind and touched the hem of His garment. ²¹For she said to herself, "If only I may touch His garment, I shall be made well." ²²But Jesus turned around, and when He saw her He said, "Be of good cheer, daughter; your faith has made you well." And the woman was made well from that hour.

—Matt. 9:20–22 (NKJV)

The woman in the scripture had been suffering from what may have seemed an incurable issue of blood for twelve years. The book of Mark states that she had been to many doctors and had spent all the money she had searching for a solution, but in spite of all she did her condition worsened. You would think by this time she would have lost hope, but the passage shows otherwise. Her faith was solid and unwavering, and she knew that by just touching the garment of Jesus, she would be healed.

Faith is the currency of heaven, and by it, miracles are obtained. Miracles are first created in the spiritual realm before they can be seen in the earth's natural realm. A person full of faith conceives the miracle in their spirit before it is visible on the earth. It is your faith that makes God incline His ear to hear your prayers and petitions and also opens His eyes to see your needs **(Heb. 11:6 NKJV)**.

> *⁵ Now when Jesus had entered Capernaum, a centurion came to Him, pleading with Him, ⁶ saying, "Lord, my servant is lying at home paralyzed, dreadfully tormented." ⁷ And Jesus said to him, "I will come and heal him." ⁸ The centurion answered and said, "Lord, I am not worthy that You should come under my roof. But only speak a word, and my servant will be healed. ⁹ For I also am a man under authority, having soldiers under me. And I say to this one, 'Go,' and he goes; and to another, 'Come,' and he comes; and to my servant, 'Do this,' and he does it." ¹⁰ When Jesus heard it, He marveled, and said to those who followed, "Assuredly, I say to you, I have not found such great faith, not even in Israel!" (Matt. 8: 5–10) NKJV*

There are different measures of faith. For instance, the Bible mentions a faith the size of a mustard seed and also a great faith like that of the centurion **(Matt. 17:20, 8:5–10 NKJV)**.

The centurion had no doubt within. His faith gave him the total confidence that Jesus could heal his servant with only speaking a word. Faith has no doubt. It doesn't reason. It's not trying to figure out the how. It only knows that Jesus will do it!

Whether through a touch or a spoken word, these two individuals obtained their miracle. Their faith made them take action. One was courageous enough to push through a crowd of people, while the other was valiant and confident in his approach. The miracle may have been manifested by different means, but the driving force that brought forth the healing miracles was the same. True faith is combined with action, and its mindset is, "If I can believe it, I will see it." Faith is the driving force that makes God respond **(Heb. 11:6)**.

Everyone has a measure of faith even people who claim to be atheists or agnostics. Some exercise it consciously and will place it on idols, finances, abilities, titles, government, doctors, etc. Others exercise it unconsciously like when getting on a plane. No one gets on a plane thinking it is not going to make it to its destination, and even though there is a slight chance of not making it, you believe it will, and that's why you get on. Every time you believe, hope, or trust in anything, you are exercising faith.

> ***And again He entered Capernaum after some days, and it was heard that He was in the house. [2] Immediately many gathered together, so that there was no longer room to receive them, not even near the door. And He preached the word to them. [3] Then they came to Him, bringing a paralytic who was carried by four men. [4] And when they could not come near Him because of the crowd, they uncovered the roof where He was. So when they had broken through, they let down the bed on which the paralytic was lying. [5] When Jesus saw their faith, He said to the paralytic, "Son, your sins are forgiven you." (Mark 2:1–5 NKJV)***

Christianity revolves around faith. The Word of God makes you aware of the power of your faith and the God who gave it and responds to it. If you are Christian and have never seen miracle, signs, and wonders, please don't feel offended, but I dare to say you are not exercising your faith to the fullest and are playing it safe. Faith makes you do radical things like the men in the scripture referenced above who, by faith, broke through the roof of a house to let down a bed with a paralytic man lying on it so that Jesus could heal him. Faith is not conservative; on the contrary, it is notable and makes a statement.

The healing of your heart, soul, and body undoubtedly depend on your faith, but not exclusively on your faith. Most importantly, your healing depends on who you place your faith on. Jesus is the only miracle worker able to heal and save your soul. If you go to Him with even faith the size of a mustard seed, He will respond to you, and His response will make your faith grow more and more each time. Faith is like a muscle, the more you exercise it, the more it grows, and the more it grows, the closer and bigger your miracles are. Dare to believe BIG! We serve a BIG GOD!

***O Lord my God, I cried out to You, And
You healed me. (Psalm 30:2 NKJV)***

CHAPTER 12

A Time to Heal

To everything there is a season, and a time for every matter or purpose under heaven: [2] A time to be born and a time to die, a time to plant and a time to pluck up what is planted, [3] A time to kill and a time to heal, a time to break down and a time to build up.

—Eccles. 3:1–3 (AMPC)

Healing is a promise from God to His children. It is your lawful right to have it! God did not intend for humanity to suffer. Pain and suffering are the results of sin and disobedience from the time of Adam and Eve and have been passed down to us through lineage.

When pain is present in a person's heart and soul, it is human nature to seek an outlet for that pain. Many will resort to alcohol, drugs, overmedicating, illicit sex, overindulgence, and so on and so forth. All these things will eventually lead to depression and desolate feelings. These quick fixes will make you feel good for a short time but will develop in you long-term addictions and dysfunctions. None of these things heal the heart and soul. More so, quick fixes are not true fixes; they only amplify and add troubles to the already troublesome, painful situation.

It is possible to process pain in a more effective, healthy, and productive way by viewing pain as a factor able to produce growth, maturity, character building, courage, and strength. When a person has a painful or disappointing experience but has a strong relationship with Jesus Christ, they are more likely to channel the pain and suffering in a positive way. This person will more than likely have a renewed mind, and because of their mental disposition they will receive peace in times of trouble, not because they don't hurt but because of what they know. They may also choose to work through the pain and embrace the process rather than numb it since there are far greater benefits for the heart and soul in doing so.

It is true that painful events change a person, for the better or worse, but if you keep your eyes on Jesus Christ and embrace that moment of pain, positive transformation is inevitable. While the transformation is happening, the heart and soul are healing. Trust and allow the process to take its course within you as there is always something greater on the other side. On the other hand, if you numb the pain, you will interrupt the processes of becoming and affect your life purpose. For instance, when a woman is giving birth to her child, the painful contraction is what helps her push the baby out into its new life. Without painful contractions, natural birth is not achievable. Just like in childbirth, pain can give you a new perspective and catapult you into your new life.

Healing is a decision that only you can make for yourself. You must acknowledge that you need and have the desire to be healed. Taking time to heal will never be wasted time; on the contrary, it is the best investment you can make for yourself, and the rewards attached to your healing will be life-changing. A healed person is a better mother, father, spouse, friend, and just a better person in general. No amount of money nor the finest things in life will do this for you. Healing is a journey personal and unique to you; it is immeasurable, so take your time and go the extra mile for yourself. Every step you take toward your healing is a step forward. The objective is to continue with forward motion since lack of motion will put you in a state of quicksand, the world is moving but you are stuck in the same place, unable to produce, become, or evolve. Being stuck is detrimental to your being and goes against the natural purpose of life. Anything living is meant to evolve, grow, and produce—it is the cycle of life. When your being is stuck, everything becomes cloudy, and you lack the ability to reach your full potential.

If you allow yourself to remain in a place of disappointment, hurt, or trauma, anything you produce from that place will be damaged. Have you ever heard the quote "Hurt people hurt people"? This quote reflects on what a wounded person will produce in others based on their heart condition.

A person that is in a state of quicksand has a damaged thought pattern, thoughts are highly influenced by experiences. Damaged thoughts will produce stereotypes and formulate inaccurate predictions. For instance, a woman who has experienced infidelity may develop trust issues and believe that all men are disloyal. This is a stereotype influenced by her experience, this is not a true statement. The reality is that there are still plenty of loyal men left in this world, but the infidelity has affected her heart and soul and in turn influenced her thoughts.

Therefore, it is necessary you apply the law of giving and receiving to your healing process—that is giving one thing in order to receive a better thing. We see this law in the life of Jesus when He laid down His life for us in exchange for the forgiveness of our sins and the salvation of our soul. This law also operates in nature. For instance, birds gradually and continuously molt their old feathers. The new feathers are stronger and better for flight, while the old damaged feathers interfere with a bird's ability to fly.

In your case, you will use God's written Word to replace your old thoughts. Don't be surprised if you find that God's Word is contrary to your current thoughts and beliefs. You must not reason or argue against it—just take it in as the absolute Truth, believe it with all your heart, and make it your reality. Meditate on God's Word as often as possible, in doing this, the Word will become engraved into the spirit of your mind, transforming, healing, and renewing your thoughts.

Like a bird when it molts its feathers, when you replace your old thoughts with God's Word, your innermost becomes stronger. As you renew your mind with the Word of God, you will notice a new and healthier way of thinking arise. Also, you will notice that the thoughts that were attached to negative experiences can no longer affect you or hold you down. As the Word of God takes permanent residency in your mind and becomes your only reality, you will easily reject opposing thoughts.

The law of giving and receiving should be applied to every area of your life whether it's giving up places you go to, people you see, or any unhealthy habits. Whatever you need to give up in exchange for your healing and a better life, do it without hesitation!

By now, you should be equipped and ready with a new mindset to embark on and conquer your new life. But it does not end there as molting is gradual and continual for birds so is evolving, growing, and producing for humans. Building "YOU" is a nonending process that should become a lifestyle. A healed person, with a changed perspective, mental awareness, and full of faith in God, can accomplish anything. "There are no limits!"

How do I know I am healed?

You will know your heart and soul are healed when the sorrowful memories you once had no longer have the power to weaken your thoughts and keep you stuck. Instead, you will regain your strength and have the desire to help others in similar situations. Once something has been processed in your mind and given a place in your heart, it loses power and can no longer torment your thoughts. You are now able to see challenges and disappointments through a new lens and are able to channel them in a healthy way.

Let's not ever forget that the heart and soul are intertwined and represent two centers. The heart is the center of your earthly life, and your soul is the center of your eternal life. They both need very special and continual care, so beware even of the little things because just a little of anything toxic can spread widely. Therefore, be very cognizant and vigilant of your entire being—spirit, soul, and body. And always, always make sure to guard your heart!

CHAPTER 13

Unveiled for Purpose

*For we are His workmanship, created in Christ
Jesus for good works, which God prepared
beforehand that we should walk in them.*

—Eph. 2:10 (NKJV)

Undoubtedly, everyone on the face of the earth was created by God, is valuable to God, and has been given a life purpose by God. There are several important factors to consider in order to find, pursue, and fulfill your life purpose.

First, you must know that your life purpose can only be revealed by God since He is the one who gave it to you and enables you to fulfill it.

Secondly, purpose cannot be fulfilled when the heart and soul are damaged. God is not going to unveil your purpose until He knows you are able to uphold it. Like in my case, I set out to find my life purpose, and instead I found the healing of my heart and soul. The salvation of your soul is very important to God and takes precedence over purpose. Jesus laid down his life in exchange for the forgiveness of our sins and the salvation of our souls. God's desire is that no one is left behind, but instead everyone be saved and live with Him in eternity.

Finally, the healing of your soul is the utmost needed preparation to walk in divine purpose. Since we produce according to our internal condition, God will make sure He cleans us up on the inside before He sends us off to fulfill our God-given purpose. God's preparation enables us to do good works and maximizes every gift and talent He has given us.

What is purpose?

> *But by the grace of God I am what I am, and His grace toward me was not in vain; but I labored more abundantly than they all, yet not I, but the grace of God which was with me. (1 Cor. 15:10 NKJV)*

Let me simplify! Think of a noun: a person, a place, or a thing. You are the person, earth is the place, and your life purpose is the thing you must find and fulfill while on your earthly journey.

Don't worry, you are not alone! God has sent His Holy Spirit to help us find our life purpose. He has also given us the natural abilities, passion, and grace to fulfill it.

Your purpose comes with an assignment(s)

Assignments are God-appointed tasks that reveal the greatness and capacity of a person.

For example: Moses was a prophet whose assignment included delivering the children of Israel from captivity by taking them out of Egypt through the wilderness toward the promised land. While Moses fulfills his assignment, he dies before the children of Israel enter the promised land.

Thereafter, Joshua, a military leader, is chosen by God to succeed Moses upon his death. He was assigned the task of taking the children of Israel into the promised land, he was to conquer the lands and distribute them among the twelve tribes. Joshua also fulfilled his assignment. These were two people with different capacities appointed at separate times to fulfill a God-given task.

When you live a purposeful life, you maximize every gift, operate in the fullness of your essence, and connect to the reason for your existence. Finding your purpose and fulfilling the assignment are what makes your being whole and your earthly journey complete.

CHAPTER 14

A Heart to Heart

For the word of God is quick, and powerful, and sharper than any two-edged sword, piercing even to the dividing asunder of soul and spirit, and of the joints and marrow, and is a discerner of the thoughts and intents of the heart.

—Heb. 4:12 (KJV)

As a young girl, I experienced many traumatic events. To start, I was separated from my father at the age of three and was raised by an abusive stepfather—a man who gave me no mercy and beat me until his hands got tired.

My mother suffered from mental illness and at times was overly medicated. She was not able to intervene, and when she tried, he would beat her as well. Her state of absence and neglect affected my childhood, adulthood, and personal development in the most negative ways. As a child, I had zero guidance and always felt very alone. Decision-making was all up to me, and as you can imagine, a child is in no capacity to dictate their own life. The results were detrimental, one bad decision led to another, causing me many hardships.

It was inevitable, rebellion set into the depths of my heart, and I became a very angry person with roller-coaster emotions. There were times I showed no mercy for others; other times I was compassionate. As a young girl, I saw friends die. I could not understand why these things happened to young people. We were supposed to be invincible happy creatures. All these experiences along with heartbreaks, betrayals, depression, anxiety, ambition, love for money—all became the destroyers of my soul.

When Jesus found me, my soul was damaged, and in His loving mercy, saved me from a life of deep darkness and isolation. It was the "engrafted Word of God" that saved my soul. Continual reading and meditating on the Word increased my faith. Soon God's Word became my reality, and I believed and continue to believe it with all my heart.

If you surrender and humble yourself before the mighty hand of God, you will be saved, healed, and transformed.

It does not matter where you find yourself. If you believe and are willing to do the work, Jesus will meet you there, and the Holy Scriptures have the power to pierce through your entire being and bring you back to a place of wholeness.

I pray this book serves as a guide for your healing journey. Remember to be patient—it's a journey. I remain a student and continue to learn daily.

The best version of YOU is in Christ Jesus!
I love you, and I'm praying for you.

Salvation Prayer
(Repeat This Prayer)

*That if you confess with your mouth the Lord Jesus
and believe in your heart that God has raised
Him from the dead, you will be saved.*

—Rom. 10:9 (NKJV)

Heavenly Father, I believe Jesus Christ died on the cross for my sins and was raised on the third day. I believe He nailed all my sins to the cross. I genuinely repent and turn away from my sins and receive Jesus Christ as my Lord and Savior. I receive my salvation by faith and know that I am loved and forgiven. In Jesus name!

Healing Prayer

*Beloved, I pray that you may prosper in all things
and be in health, just as your soul prospers.*

—3 John 1:2 (NKJV)

Heavenly Father, I pray for my precious friends and bring them before Your throne of grace and mercy. I pray that You partner with them as they continue their healing journey. I pray You fill them with strength, joy, and peace and reveal Yourself to them daily even in the small things, Lord. I pray that You capture their heart and make your thoughts their thoughts. I pray You pour healing balm over every wound in their soul and mend their broken heart. I pray that at the end of their journey, they will be healed, changed, and prospered. In Jesus name! Amen!

Closing Prayer

Dear Lord, the same way You pulled my soul out of darkness and made your word a lamp to my feet and a light to my path, I ask that You do the same for my readers and friends.

Lord, when they feel lost and have no sense of direction, shine your light on them and highlight the path they are to walk on. Take them by the hand and order each of their steps. Give them deer feet so they do not fall into the enemy's traps. Embrace, love, uphold them in each of their struggles, and help them to always find their way.

Lord, when they feel weak, You make them strong. You renew their strengths, give them wings like eagles, and help them to run and not be weary and to walk and not faint.

Most importantly Lord, keep them safe in the palm of Your hand for all the days of their lives, and help them to endure the race with peace and joy in their hearts. In Jesus name, I pray. Amen!

ABOUT THE AUTHOR

Arlette Tejeda, the author, was born in Havana, Cuba, and arrived in Miami Beach, Florida, at the age of three where she resided for most of her life. She recently traded in the Florida beaches for the Rocky Mountains—Colorado is her new home.

Arlette prides herself in being the mother of three amazing children and is also extremely proud of being a grandmother. She considers her family to be one of the greatest gifts God has given her—a gift that keeps giving. As is the case, Arlette is currently overwhelmed with excitement waiting for her second grandchild.

For over a decade now, Arlette has been diligent in answering the call of God on her life and does so by serving the body of Christ in different capacities. One of the many areas of service has been partaking in street evangelism where she has experienced the supernatural power of God many times, supported by miracles, signs, and wonders. Her desire is to see people saved, healed, and transformed by the transformative love and power of God.